Irmgard Kneissler

Origami

A children's book

illustrations by Dieter Jonas
and
photography by Max Schwendt

 CHILDRENS PRESS®
CHICAGO

Translation by Mrs. Werner Lippmann and Mrs. Ruth Bookey

Library of Congress Cataloging-in-Publication Data

Kneissler, Irmgard.
    [Origami Kinderbuch. English]
    Origami/by Irmgard Kneissler; illustrated by Dieter Jonas.
        p. cm.
    Translation of: Origami Kinderbuch.
    Summary: Includes step-by-step directions for creating a variety
of origami, or folded paper, projects.
    ISBN 0-516-09261-8
    1. Origami—Juvenile literature. [1. Origami. 2. Handicraft.]
I. Jonas, Dieter, ill. II. Title.
TT870.K57313   1992
736'.982—dc20   92-453
                                                       CIP
                                                       AC

Published in the United States in 1992 by Childrens Press®, Inc.,
5440 North Cumberland Avenue, Chicago, IL 60656.

Copyright © 1992, 1987 Ravensburger Buchverlag Otto Maier GmbH, Germany.
Originally published in West Germany under the title *Das kannst du auch.*
        3 4 5 6 7 8 9 0 R 01 00 99 98 97 96 95 94 93

Contents

ntroduction

You've probably built houses with blocks. Maybe you've even used blocks that look like parts of real buildings, such as doors and windows. Building plans are usually included with the blocks. These plans are helpful for a beginning builder. But the real fun begins when you start developing your own ideas. If they are not too successful at first, you try again, very carefully. What does building with blocks have to do with origami? *Origami* is a Japanese word that means "the art of paper-folding." Over the years the Japanese have developed and refined the techniques of origami, as a house-builder refines techniques to build better houses and a vast variety of types of houses.

Once you learn the basic origami plans, you can try ideas of your own for folding paper. Origami is a way of playing with paper, but you must be very careful and exact when you fold, or the figures will not come out.

Do not start reading this book in the middle. Start at the very beginning. If you follow the directions step-by-step, you too can become a master of origami.

Paper

There are many kinds of paper, but not all are good for origami. Newspaper would be too thick for folding small shapes. Tissue paper wrinkles too easily. Crepe paper does not keep its shape. Construction paper rips and breaks in the folds. Paper napkins are too thin. Typing paper and some notebook papers are good for folding, but the very best paper is the paper made especially for origami. Origami paper is colored on one side and white on the other. It holds its shape very well, and it is already square, the shape that most origami starts with.

To make a square from a rectangular piece of paper, follow the drawings below. Be sure to fold the paper very carefully so that your paper is exactly square.

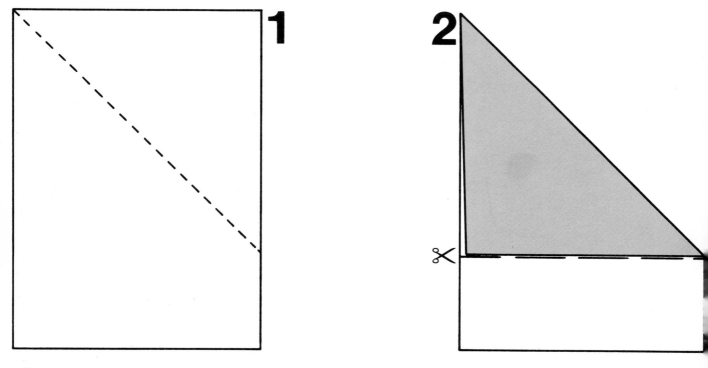

This page shows you how to cut a square from an irregular piece of paper.

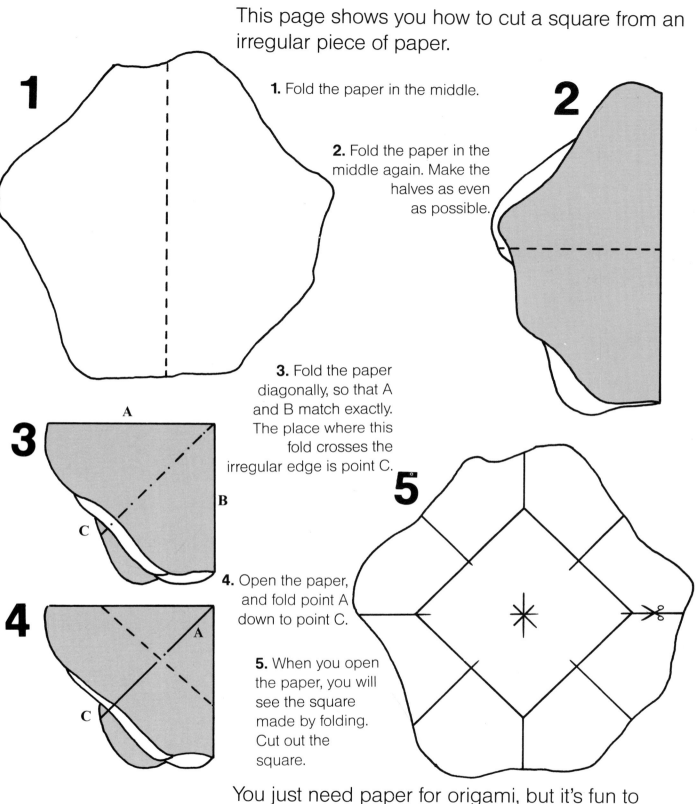

1

1. Fold the paper in the middle.

2

2. Fold the paper in the middle again. Make the halves as even as possible.

3

A

B

C

3. Fold the paper diagonally, so that A and B match exactly. The place where this fold crosses the irregular edge is point C.

4

A

C

4. Open the paper, and fold point A down to point C.

5

5. When you open the paper, you will see the square made by folding. Cut out the square.

You just need paper for origami, but it's fun to decorate the finished shapes. Make drawings with crayons or felt-tip pens. Or glue on some bows, stars, etc.

The Drawings

Origami is not as difficult as it looks. Like learning read, you learn one step at a time, until it become second nature. Every origami figure starts with on basic shape. Detailed drawings show you how to make each new shape as it is introduced.

On the following pages, the drawings show where you should fold. Follow them as if they were a ma Look at drawings 1 and 2 on page 9. The dotted line on drawing 1 shows where you should fold. Drawing 2 shows how it should look when it's dor

In the beginning, put the paper on the table, white side up, and mark the corners A, B, C, and D right the paper. This will make it easier. There are many different origami folds, and they are shown in the drawings throughout this book. Wherever you see broken lines on a drawing (- - - -), fold the paper toward the front—this is a "valley fold." Wherever yo see dotted lines (· · · ·), fold the paper toward the back—a "mountain fold." A broken dotted line (- · - · - · - or - · · · -) is a crease. That's easy to remember. But if you should forget, look in the ba of this book for explanations of origami vocabulary

The drawings show which way you should lay the paper down. Although you can turn your paper as often as you wish, when you are ready to fold, lay it down the way it is shown in the drawing. Soon you will be able to try out your own ideas, and origami will really be fun for you.

The Basic Triangle Shape

Every origami figure starts with one basic shape. Each new basic shape in the following pages has an explanation with it. Later, you will not need long explanations. The drawings will be enough. But when we come to a new shape or a more difficult figure, an explanation will be provided.

1. For the triangle shape, you need a square of paper. Lay the paper on the table, colored side down, exactly as shown in the drawing. Point A should be on top, pointing away from you. Point C should be on the bottom, pointing toward you. Make a valley fold on the broken line. (Always fold broken lines toward you.) You can fold corner A down to meet C, or you can fold corner C up to meet A.

Now look at drawing 2. Corner A has been folded down to meet C. Note that there is a circle around C. This shows that C will be under A (and not visible when the paper is folded properly).

2. This double triangle is a basic shape.

1

A

B

C

2

D

B

A Ⓒ

Hand Puppets

This is a basic pattern that you can fold and color, as the pictures show. The pig is only one of the many animals you can fold from this basic pattern.

The Pig has a fat head, pointed ears, and a square snout! Here are the drawings and directions:

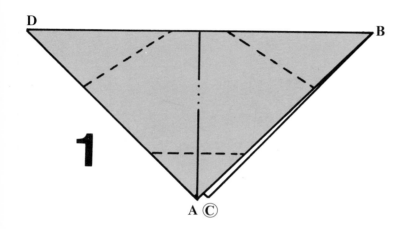

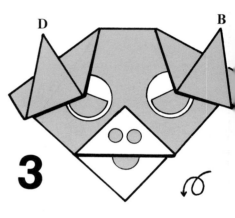

1. Starting with the basic triangle, fold corners B and D together at the back along the center dotted line (mountain fold). Crease, and then unfold. Points B and D are no longer corners of the big triangle. They look like points, and we will call them points.

Now fold B and D down on the broken lines (valley fold), and fold point A up. Look at point A in drawing 2 to see exactly how it's folded up to form the mouth. Decide how big you want the mouth.

2. Make valley folds to fold points B and D up as in drawing 3. Points B and D will become the ears. You can make them long or short, but make sure they are even.

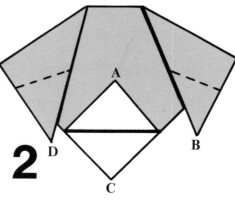

3. This is your first origami figure. Draw the eyes, nose, and mouth with crayons.

4. Cut a slit for your fingers in the back of the pig. If you want the pig to open its mouth, fold A down and C up. Hold the pig with a thumb and index finger where the X's are. Move your fingers back and forth.

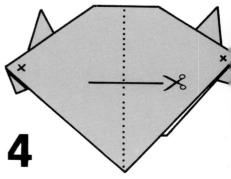

You can use the basic triangle shape to make animal heads of many shapes and sizes. You can fold points B and D to the front or the back, up or down. But since we are just getting started, we'll stay with this basic pattern and look at its many possibilities.

Poodle and Cat

The Poodle has long ears and a wide face. You already recognize the shape in drawing 1, so no explanation will be given.

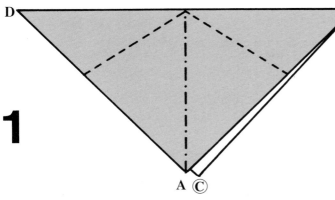

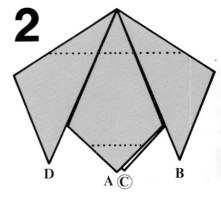

1. Fold the triangle in half (bring points B and D together), crease, and open. Fold points B and D down as shown in drawing 2.
2. Now fold the top dotted line away from you—a mountain fold. (Drawing 3 shows how it should look.) You could turn the paper around and fold the other way. But be sure you turn it around again before you do the next step. Fold A and C up separately toward the inside of the figure. Make sure the folds are even.

The Cat has a wide, triangular, pointed head. The ears are at the edges of the head.

After you crease the center line, fold points A and C down together. Then fold points B and D up on the broken lines. Now turn the figure over. Draw a cat face with crayons or felt-tip pens.

To use this head as a puppet, glue tips AC and the ears, so that the head won't come apart when you stick your finger in it.

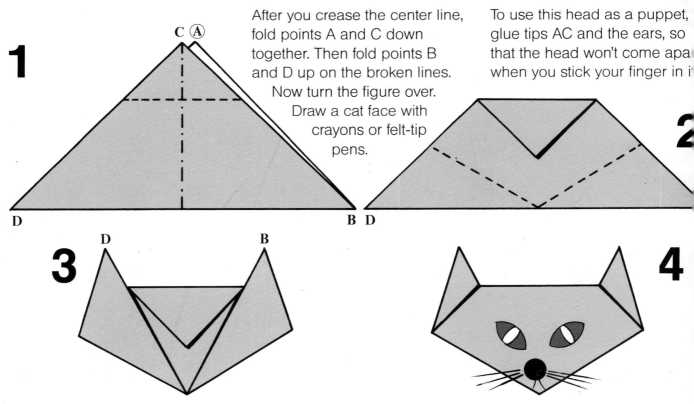

Elephant

The Elephant has two large ears and a trunk, so you will need three points instead of two. We will show you how to do this by drawing and folding "helper" lines (see drawings 1 and 2). Point E must be exactly on the X in drawing 3.

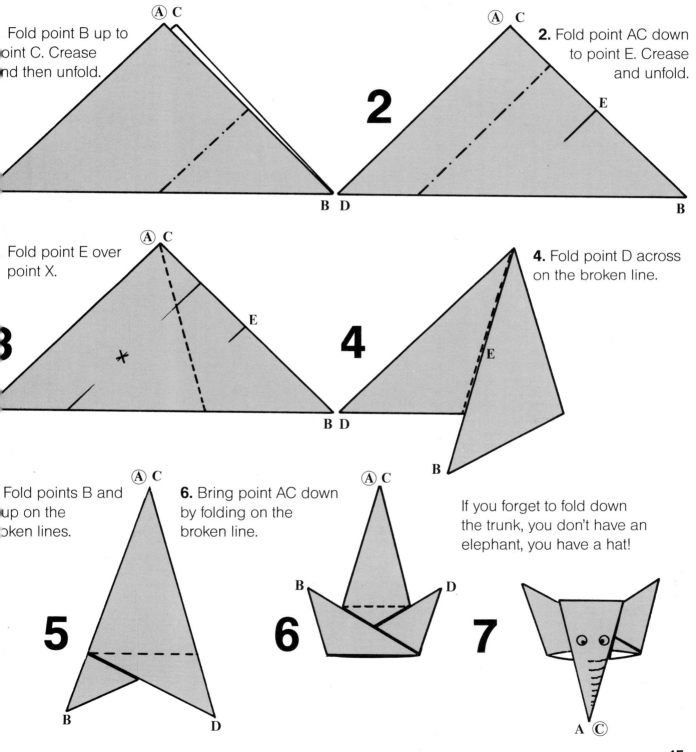

Fold point B up to point C. Crease and then unfold.

2. Fold point AC down to point E. Crease and unfold.

2

Fold point E over point X.

4. Fold point D across on the broken line.

4

Fold points B and up on the ken lines.

6. Bring point AC down by folding on the broken line.

If you forget to fold down the trunk, you don't have an elephant, you have a hat!

5

6

7

Sailboat Race

Here is a party game that can be played on a slippery floor or tabletop. The floor or the tabletop serves as the water. You make the sailboats. Use a different color for each boat and glue on a small flag. Name the boats. When you are folding the basic boat form, put the white side of the paper face-up, and you will have a white boat with a colorful sail. To race your fleet, put one boat in front of each person (on the floor or table) and blow your sailboat to victory.

1. Fold up on the broken line. First, check drawing 3 so you can see where point C will end up.

2. Unfold, leaving creases as shown in 2. White side up, make mountain folds along ED and EB. Folds AE and EC will fall into place.

3. One at a time, fold D and B inward to look like drawing 4.

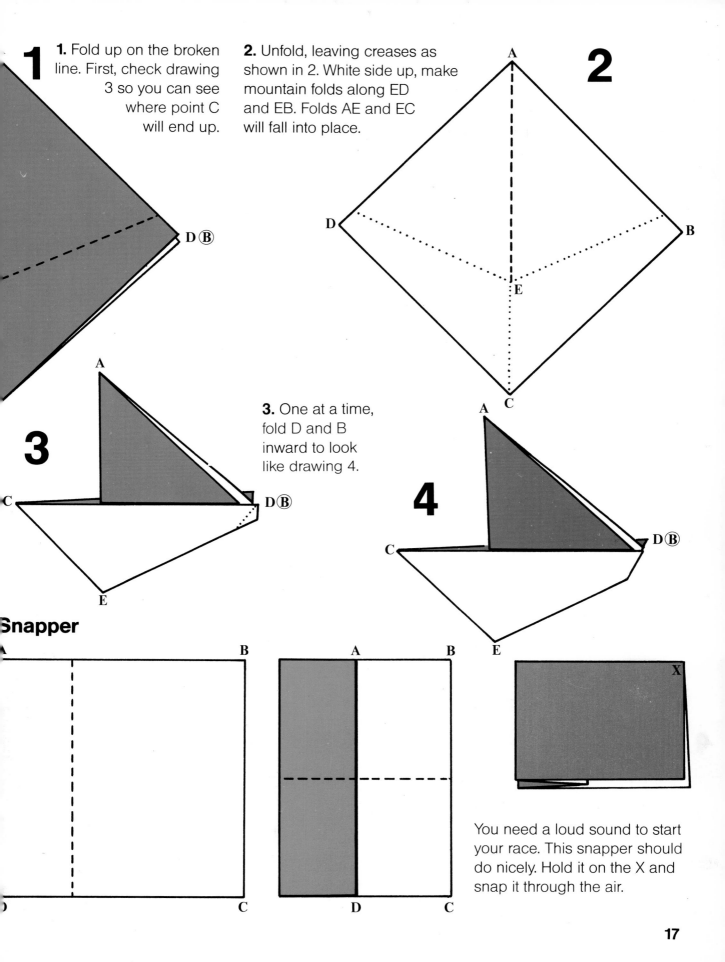

D Ⓑ

A

B

D

E

C

1

2

3

A

C

E

D Ⓑ

4

A

C

E

D Ⓑ

Snapper

A   B

D   C

A   B

D   C

X

You need a loud sound to start your race. This snapper should do nicely. Hold it on the X and snap it through the air.

17

Advanced Folding—Jet Plane

Paper folding is mentioned in a Japanese story written over one thousand years ago. At that time, the Western world had not even heard of paper. Paper folding is a folk art in Japan, and almost everyone can do it. The Japanese are constantly folding new figures, not just the old standbys. This jet plane is a new figure. Look at the drawings carefully. Only step 6 has directions and explanations.

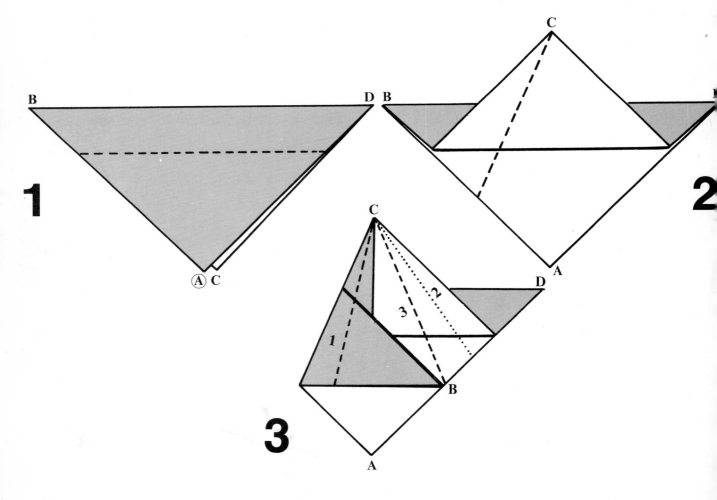

4

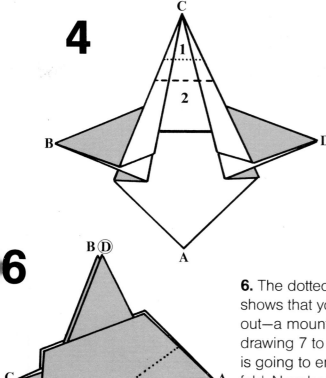

5

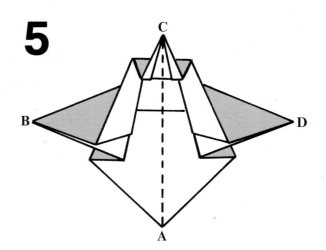

6

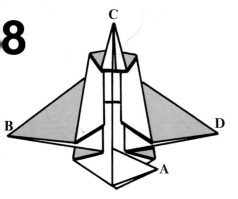

6. The dotted line in drawing 6 shows that you need to fold out—a mountain fold. Look at drawing 7 to see where point A is going to end up. Open this fold. Now bend it the other way to make a valley fold. Now push point A up between the two halves in a mountain fold (see drawing 7). Fold along the dotted line in drawing 7, and then open the wings.

7

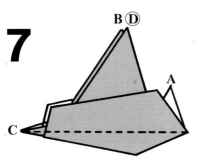

8

Useful Things

Some people prefer to make useful things. The basic triangle shape is good for this. So far we have emphasized the corners and edges of the paper in folding to get our figures. These next examples fold in on themselves. This strengthens the figures in the center. The cup is one of the oldest origami shapes. It is an easy shape to fold. This cup is practical and lasting. You can drink from it. If you make one large enough, you can use it as a hat. Newspaper is good for hats.

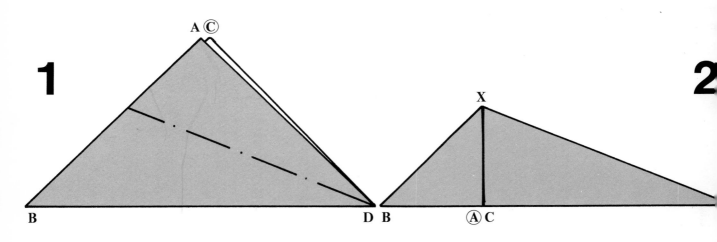

1. Fold the basic triangle shape. Now make a fold on the line shown in drawing 1, bringing corners A and C down to the base of the triangle. Look at drawing 2 to see what it should look like.

2. Open the fold. Notice point X.

3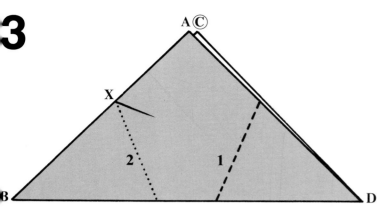

4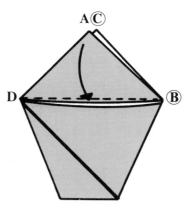

3. Remember that a broken line is a valley fold, one that's folded toward you. A dotted line indicates a mountain fold, folded away from you. Fold point D with a valley fold to point X and point B with a mountain fold toward the back to the newly created corner. Turn your figure over to make sure the folds are even. Then turn it back and study drawing 4.

4. Push point A down inside the flap that was made by folding point D across in front.

5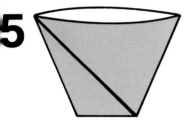

5. Push point C down inside the flap made by folding point B across the back. Now you have a cup.

With one or two easy changes in the folding, you can create a new origami figure.

The Coin Holder is made in almost the same way as the cup. Only this time corners B and D are both folded toward the front, and corner A is folded into the opening. Fold point C into the same opening and you can close the top. Fold a larger version with heavier paper, do not fold point C in, and hang the figure on the wall as a container (see drawing 3).

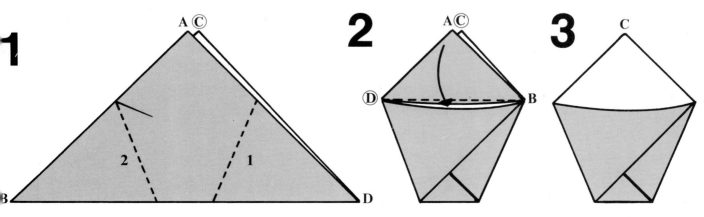

A Small Basket starts with step 4 of the cup (see page 23). Cut along the line where you see the scissors in drawing 2 below. Then tuck in the remainder of flaps A and C as you did for the cup.

1

2

3

4

Hat Parade

The basic cup shape can be used to make various hats. Turn the cup shape upside down and you have a Turkish fez. You can make a tall, pointed hat out of the elephant (see page 15). Create tiny hats for your fingers. You can probably come up with your own ideas, but first try the hats below.

1. Fold the cup as far as step 4 (see page 23). Turn the whole thing around and fold point A up behind, and point C up in front.

2. Hold the hat by corners B and D. Bring B and D together, so that D is on top of B. Now push point X inward toward the center of the hat's top, so that point F will lie on top of point E. Make sure all folds are flat before you open the hat.

1. Fold the hat. Now fold corners D and B toward the front and back, respectively, on the broken line.

2. Hold points A and C and pull apart.

Fold the coin holder (page 23). Turn it around. Fold corner C up and down again, as indicated by the broken lines.

Hat

Admiral's Hat

Knight's Helmet

3. Fold as shown in drawing 2 for the first hat above.

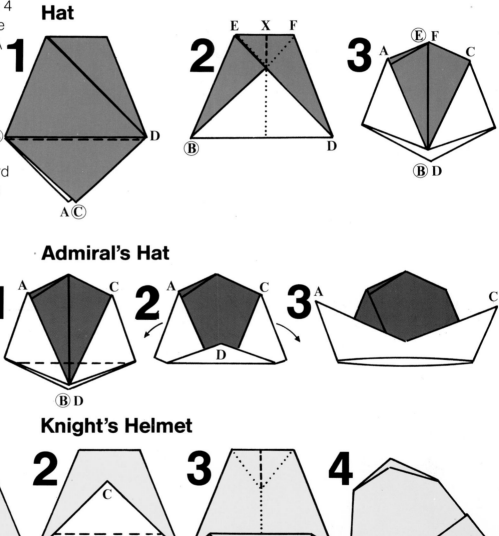

Samurai Helmet

1

1. Fold the basic triangle shape. Fold on the broken dotted line. Crease firmly and open up again. Make a mountain fold on the dotted line. Or, turn the paper around, make a valley fold on the dotted line, and turn the paper back again.

2

2. Make valley folds on the broken lines bringing points D and B down toward AC.

4

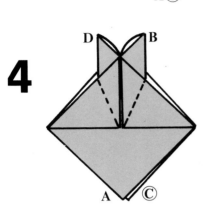

4. Make valley folds on the broken lines. Points D and B will now look like drawing 5. (Tip: Never fold while holding the paper in the air. Always fold on a firm surface.) Now look at the next drawing.

5

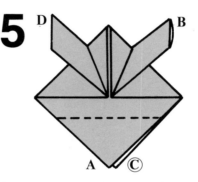

5. Fold corner A up on the broken line.

3

3. Fold points B and D up on the broken line.

8

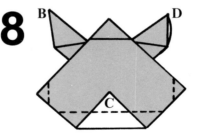

8. All broken lines in drawing 8 will be valley folds.

9. Lines 1 and 2 in drawing 9 are valley folds.

6

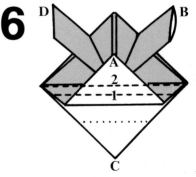

6. First make a valley fold on broken line 1. Then make another valley fold on broken line 2. Fold point C toward the back on the dotted line.

7

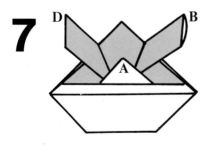

7. Turn your work over. Up to now you have worked on the front of the helmet.

9

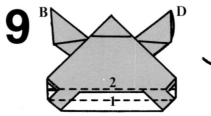

Advanced Folding

Rabbit Hat. You will recognize the beginning figure (see page 26, drawing 5). Follow the drawings on this page to make the rabbit hat.

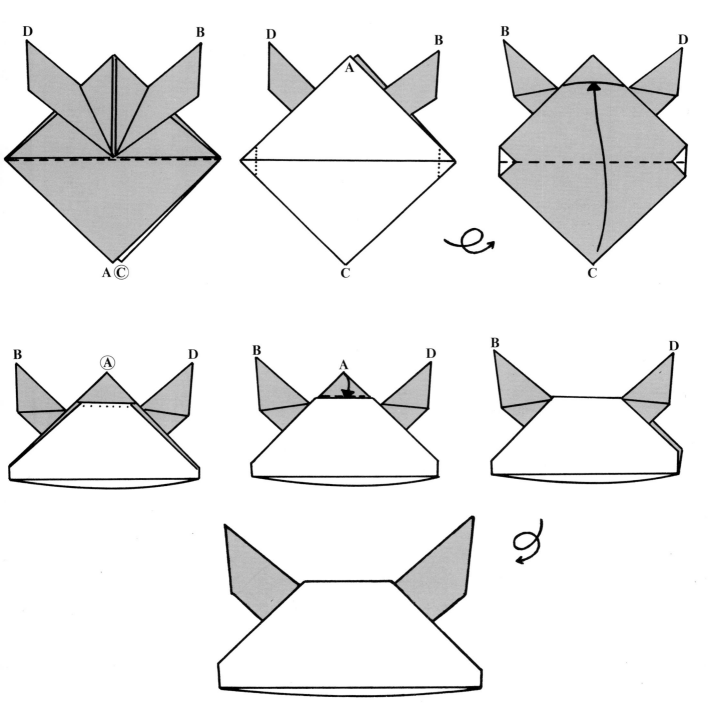

Basic Kite Shape

First fold the triangle shape, crease the fold, and open the paper. Fold two diagonal "helper" lines toward the middle crease. Fold point A and point C to the middle crease (valley fold). This is the basic kite shape.

1

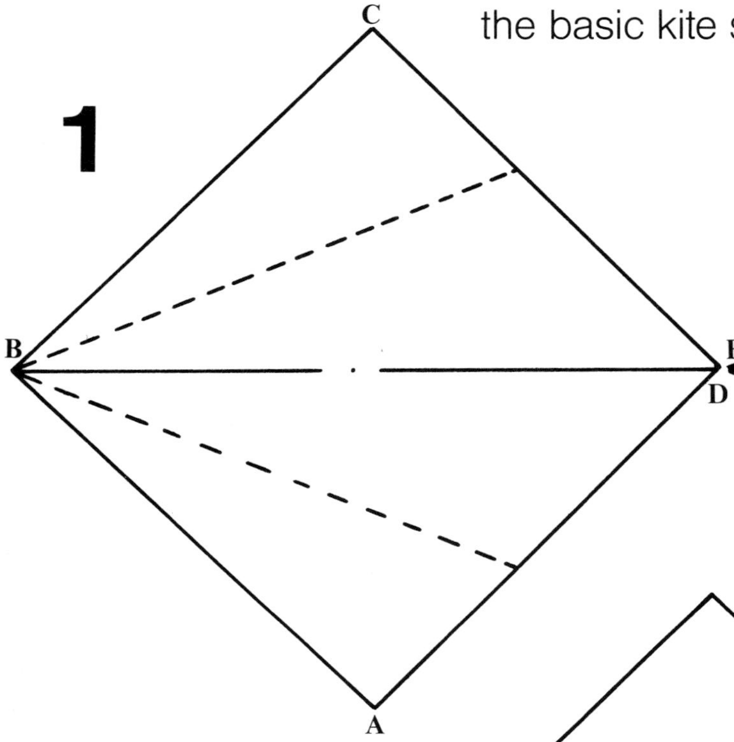

2

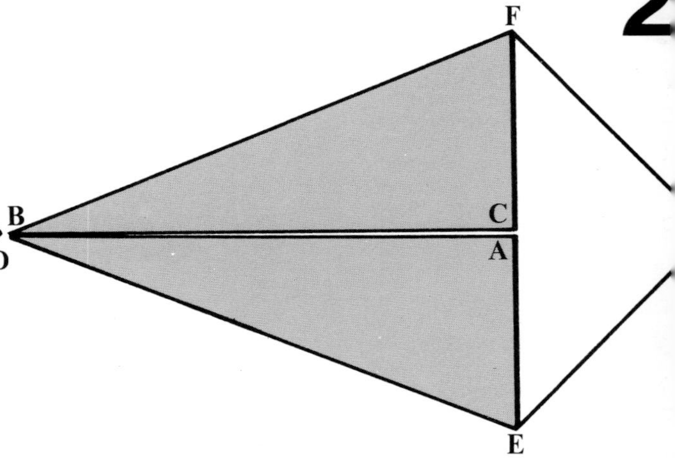

Attach a long, thin thread or string, as shown in drawing 3. Attach a tail, then take your kite outside and see if it will fly. The best kites are made out of heavier paper.

3

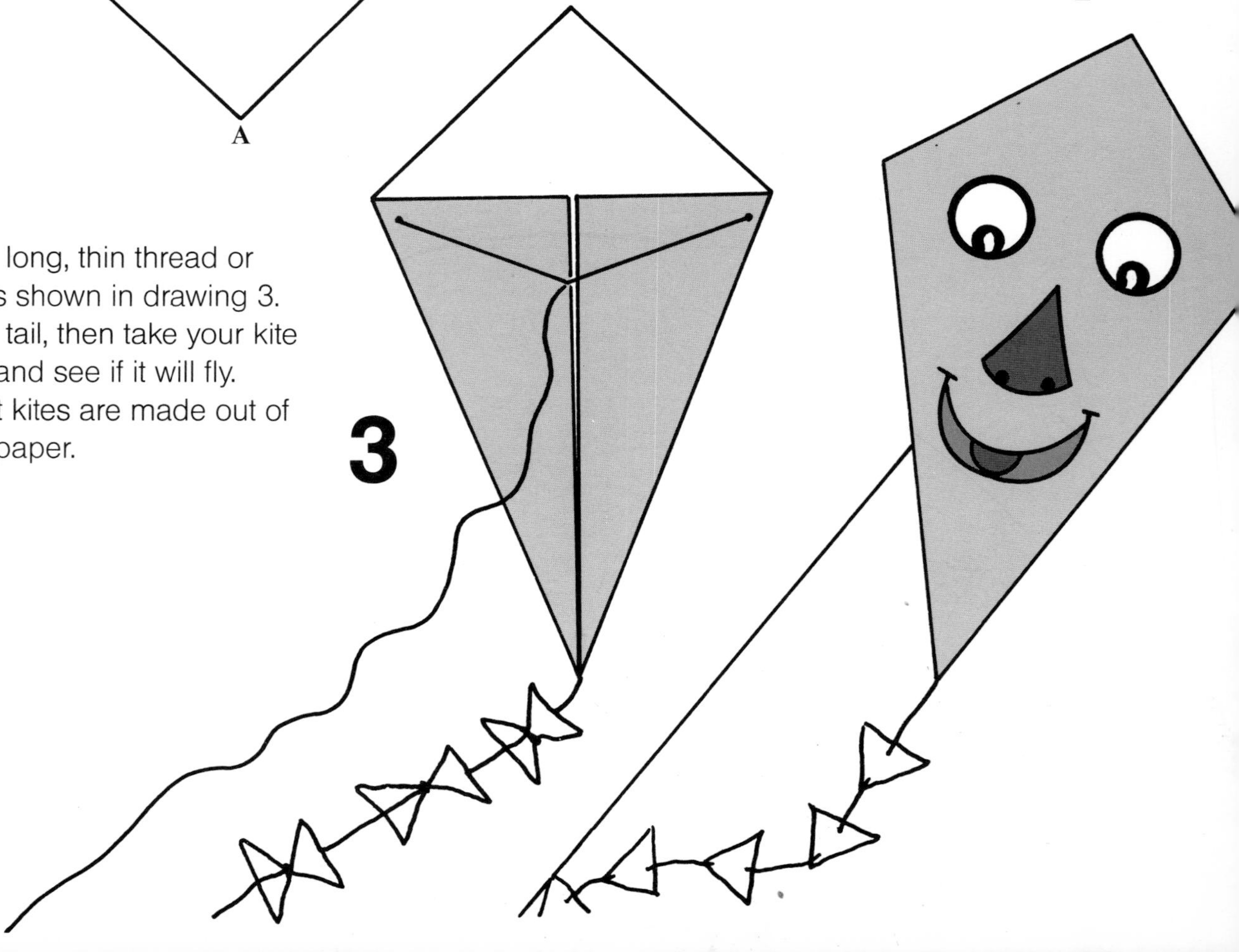

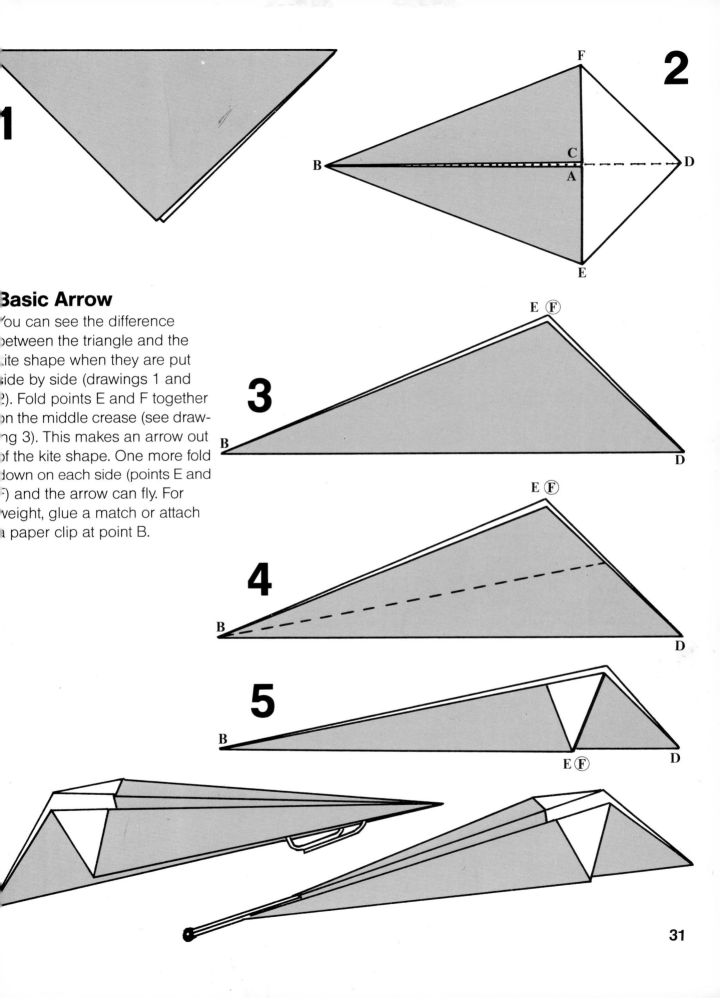

1

2

Basic Arrow

You can see the difference between the triangle and the kite shape when they are put side by side (drawings 1 and 2). Fold points E and F together on the middle crease (see drawing 3). This makes an arrow out of the kite shape. One more fold down on each side (points E and F) and the arrow can fly. For weight, glue a match or attach a paper clip at point B.

3

4

5

Birds and More Birds

The basic bird shape can be folded into a variety of bird forms.

To fold these birds, you need origami paper, a large piece of white paper, crayons, and construction paper. You don't need long explanations this time. Simply fold the basic kite shape into an arrow (see drawing at left). Then fold the point in different directions and at different places to make longer or shorter heads. Glue your birds on the white paper to create a bird world. Draw legs and eyes to give your birds character.

Starting with this basic beginning shape, you can fold many different kinds of heads, tails, and wings. See the drawings.

Reverse Folding   Origami Trick

Reverse folding can change your origami birds in wonderful ways. Reverse folding can be done toward the inside of your bird or toward the outside. This sort of folding can be done only if there is a center fold.

The Crow is an easy shape on which to practice reverse folding.

1

1. First fold the basic kite shape. Make a valley fold in the center and fold the arrow shape.

2a

2. Fold point B down to the desired length (drawing 2a). You will have a valley fold in front and a mountain fold in back. Open the fold (see drawing 2b). Turn the valley fold into a mountain fold (drawing 2) and crease. Now fold

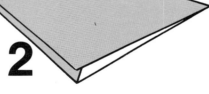

2

inward along the line from B to X, along the crease, as shown in drawing 3.

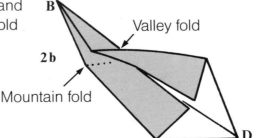

Valley fold

2b

Mountain fold

3

For this figure, reverse folding is done toward the inside. Practice this. It will work only if you first fold toward the outside as shown in drawing 2a. The crease is shown as a dotted line because the fold inside will give you a mountain fold on both sides of the figure. Be sure to study the drawings closely. They will show if you should make a regular mountain fold or a reverse fold. A mistake is easily corrected. Just smooth out the paper and refold it.

The Duck is an easy figure to make to practice reverse folding.

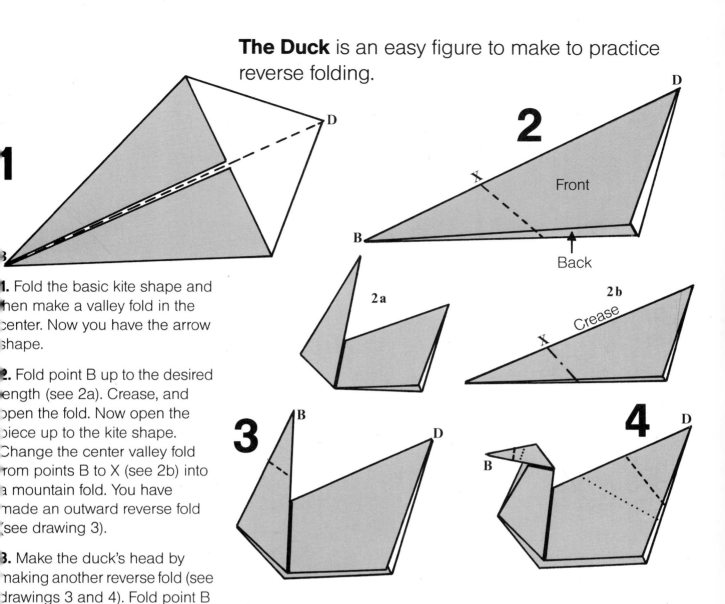

1. Fold the basic kite shape and then make a valley fold in the center. Now you have the arrow shape.

2. Fold point B up to the desired length (see 2a). Crease, and open the fold. Now open the piece up to the kite shape. Change the center valley fold from points B to X (see 2b) into a mountain fold. You have made an outward reverse fold (see drawing 3).

3. Make the duck's head by making another reverse fold (see drawings 3 and 4). Fold point B down, crease, and open. Now make a reverse fold (see drawing 4). Study the drawings carefully.

4. The folding of the beak and tail is more difficult. Fold and crease along the dotted lines and the broken lines in drawing 4. For the tail, open the figure and hold it with the duck's back facing toward you. Make a mountain fold along the longer crease (dotted line), and a valley fold along the shorter crease (broken line).

5. Turn the figure around so that the duck's head is facing you. Make the same kinds of folds for the beak.

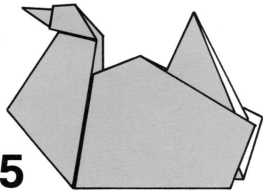

This more difficult kind of folding is the basis for advanced origami folding. After you have done it a few times, it will become easy.

The Fish Shape

The basic kite shape is also the beginning of the fish shape. This shape can be varied. Because the fish is new, we will include more directions.

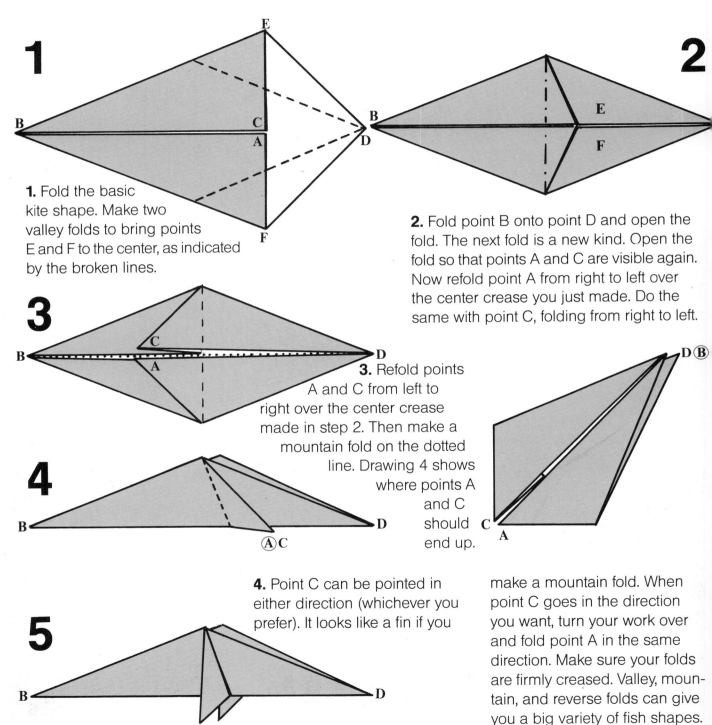

1. Fold the basic kite shape. Make two valley folds to bring points E and F to the center, as indicated by the broken lines.

2. Fold point B onto point D and open the fold. The next fold is a new kind. Open the fold so that points A and C are visible again. Now refold point A from right to left over the center crease you just made. Do the same with point C, folding from right to left.

3. Refold points A and C from left to right over the center crease made in step 2. Then make a mountain fold on the dotted line. Drawing 4 shows where points A and C should end up.

4. Point C can be pointed in either direction (whichever you prefer). It looks like a fin if you make a mountain fold. When point C goes in the direction you want, turn your work over and fold point A in the same direction. Make sure your folds are firmly creased. Valley, mountain, and reverse folds can give you a big variety of fish shapes.

Advanced Folding

The kite shape can be folded into many shapes, including the one on this page. How about trying some of your own ideas with this basic shape?

The Standing Mouse. The mouse's head is very heavy, so when you push its tail down and then let go, it will fall right down on its head again.

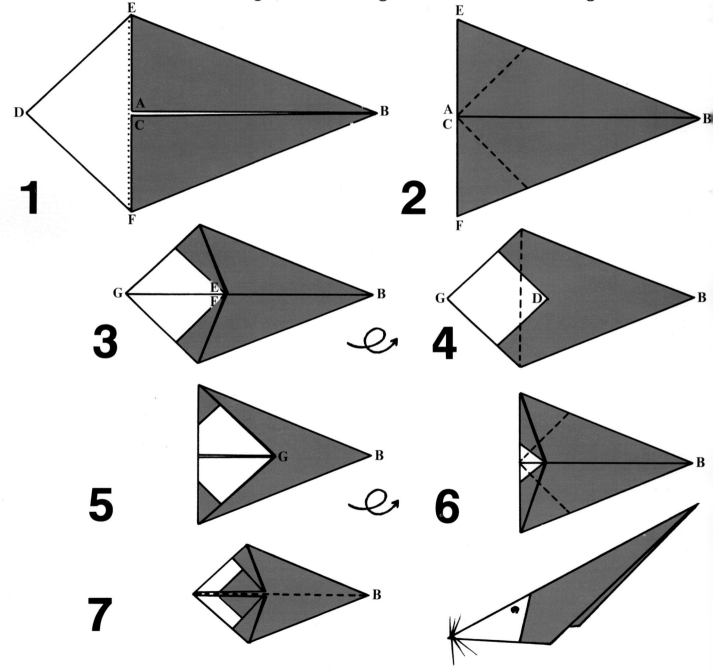

Basic Book Shape

The name says it! Fold your paper in the exact middle, so it will open like a book. This basic shape is as simple as the triangle. With this shape, you can make a whole new set of figures.

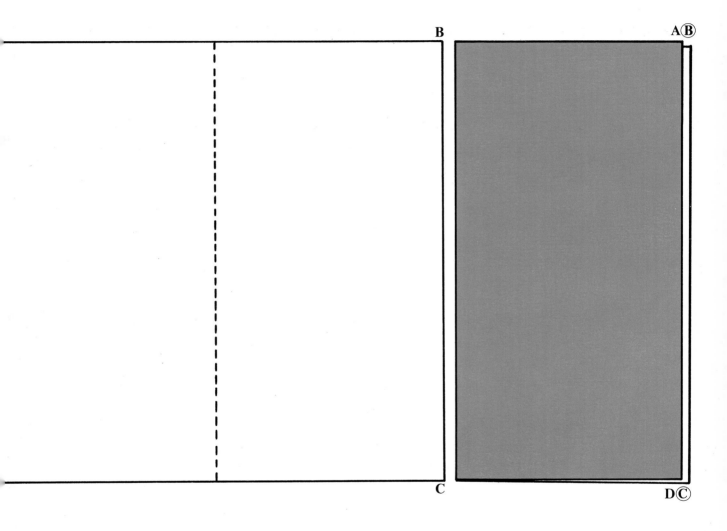

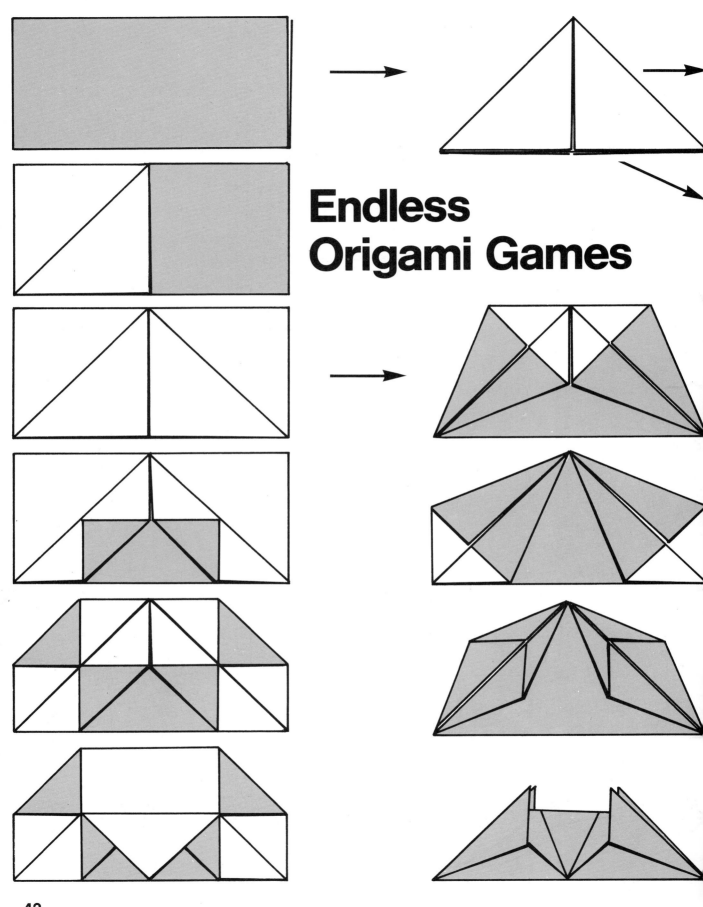

Endless
Origami Games

It's fun to fold geometric patterns. Each time you fold toward the back, the front, the inside, the outside, diagonally, or straight, a new pattern unfolds. This is a game with endless possibilities. It's perfect for a rainy-day activity.

The book shape is particularly good for folding geometric patterns. Always fold toward the middle crease. After you make the fold, crease it and then open the paper. Now you have another pattern.

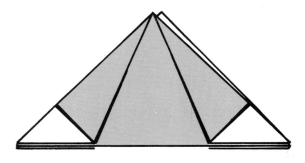

You can vary the pattern by changing the side of the paper, colored or white, you use when you fold.

On the previous page the folds were made toward the center crease. You can also fold toward the edge of the paper. Close off the open side, and create a sort of bag. This bag shape is very good for making hats. If you unfold your paper, you will have good line designs that can be colored in or cut out.

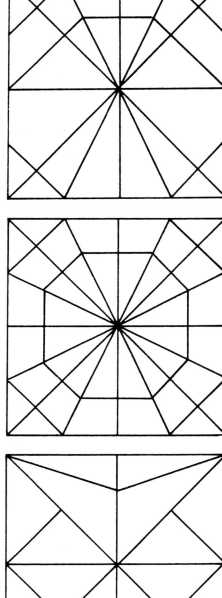

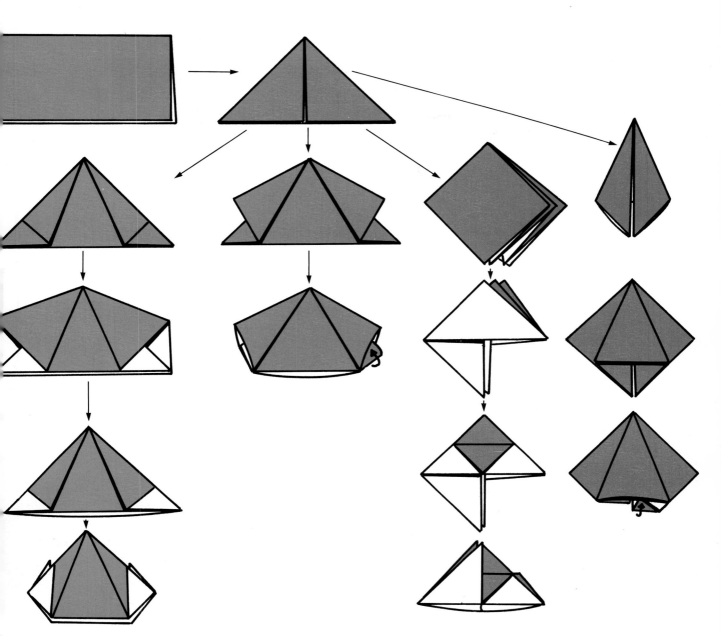

You can fold paper puzzles using two sheets of origami paper.

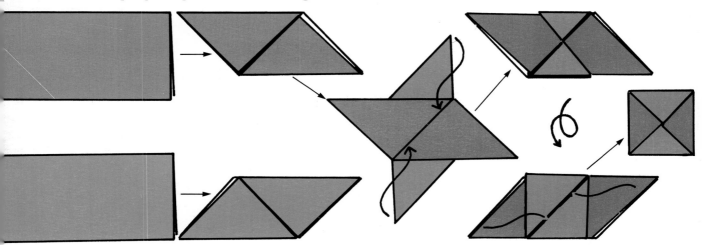

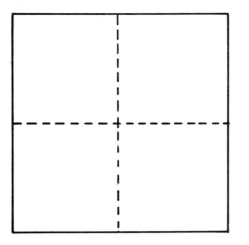

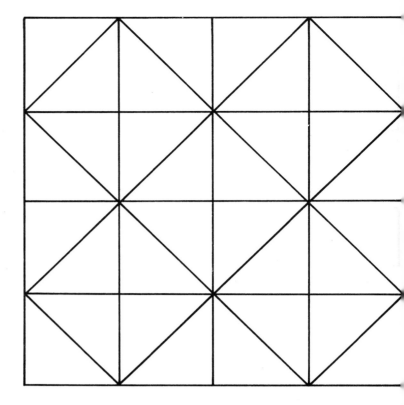

The middle crease is very important when you start folding from the basic book shape. Fold middle creases in both directions, for helper lines. In these examples most of the folding is done toward these middle creases. Note the X's in the bottom drawings: put a finger under each point marked X, open, and fold down.

You can make hats and pockets with this way of folding.

Open your work and go over the creases. See how neat your folding is.

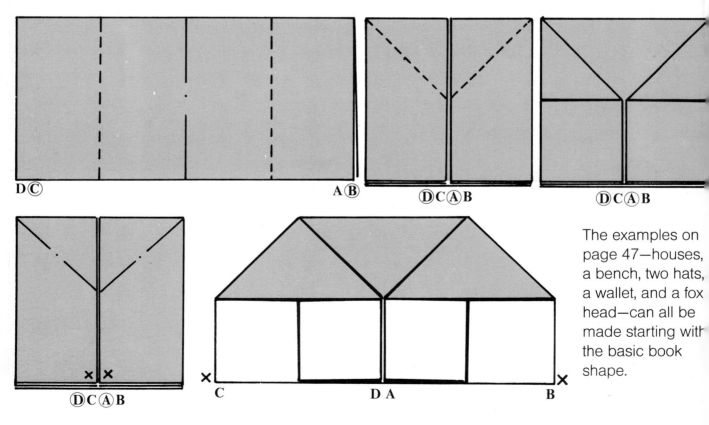

D Ⓒ

Aⓑ

ⒹCⒶB

ⒹCⒶB

ⒹCⒶB

× ×

× C   D A   B ×

The examples on page 47—houses, a bench, two hats, a wallet, and a fox head—can all be made starting with the basic book shape.

46

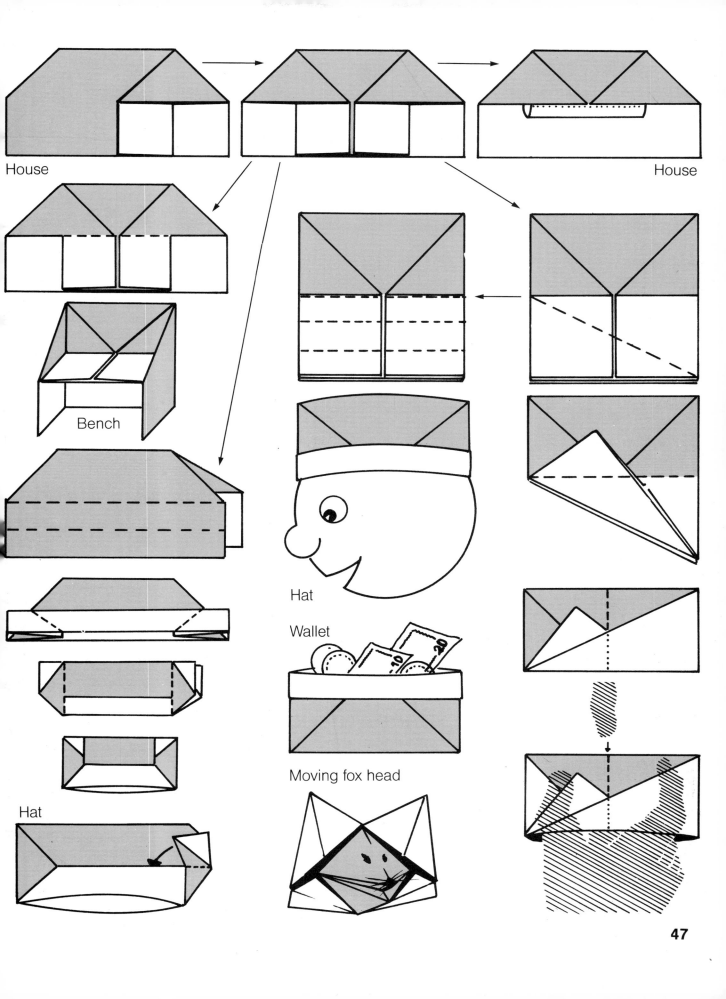

House

House

Bench

Hat

Hat

Wallet

Moving fox head

47

After folding and creasing the middle fold, open the paper and use the middle crease as a guide. See the drawings on this page. Use rectangular paper for the train engine, railroad car, and the houses. In making the train and the cars, you will use many reverse folds. Follow the drawings carefully. For the cars, you will learn a new way of folding.

Watch for reverse folds. Here, they start as valley folds.

House

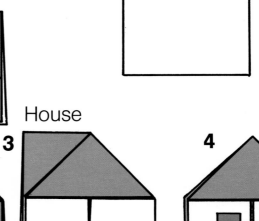

1 Train engine

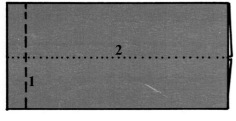

1 Railroad car

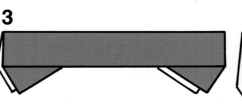

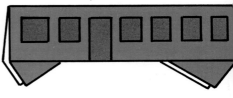

1 Automobile

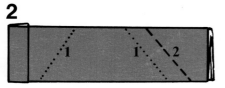

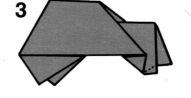

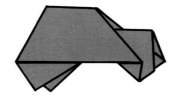

Watch for reverse folds. Here, they start as valley folds.

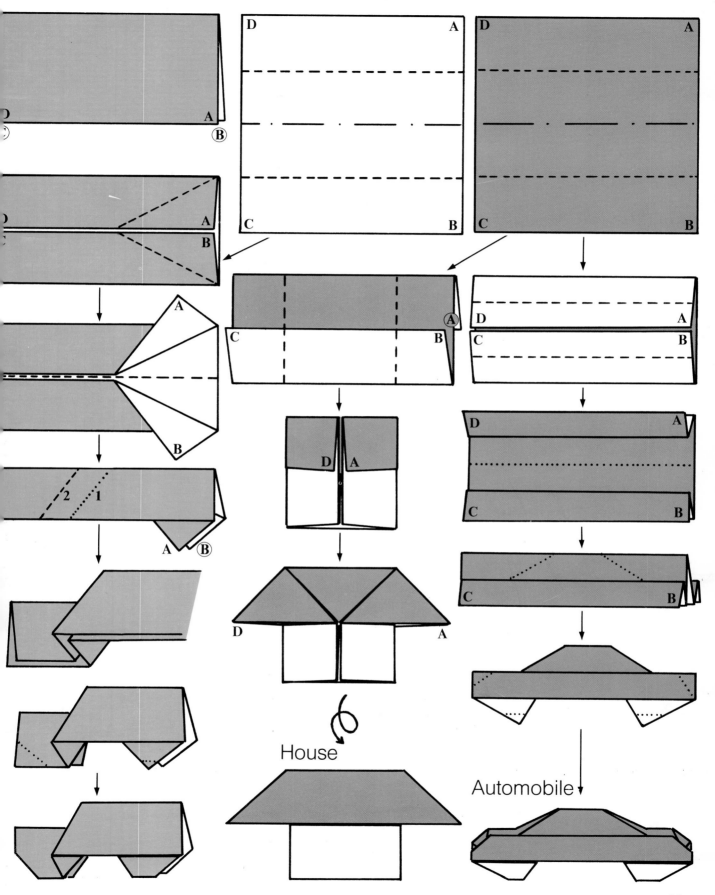

House

Automobile

49

Arrow

Start with the basic book shape. Look at the drawings and you will recognize the folds. This arrow flies fast to its target.

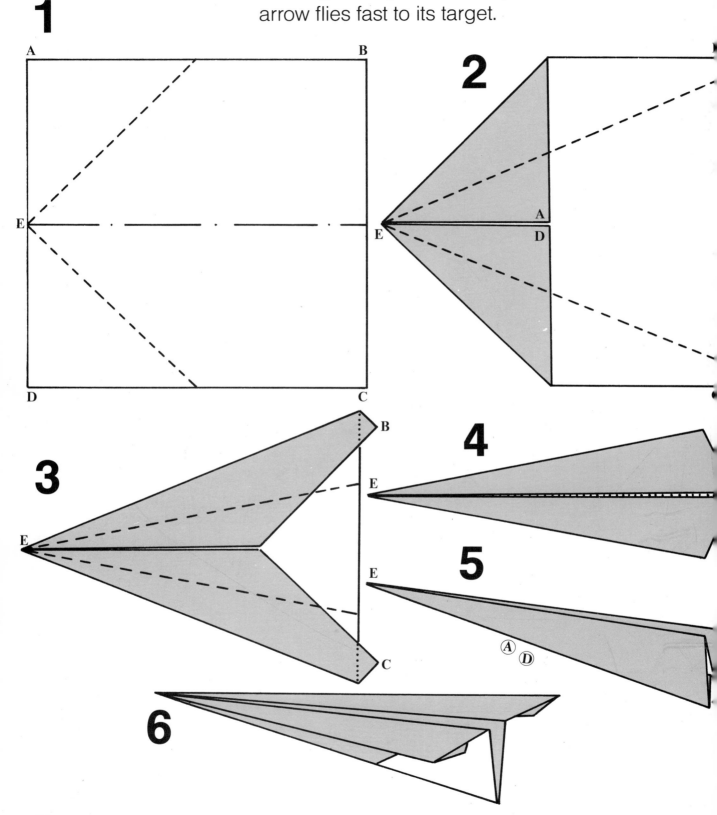

Airplane

This will not be difficult. It is a good example of another variation. Follow the directions for the arrow as far as drawing 2 on page 50. Then fold corner E as shown on this page (drawing 1). Then follow the drawings below to complete the figure.

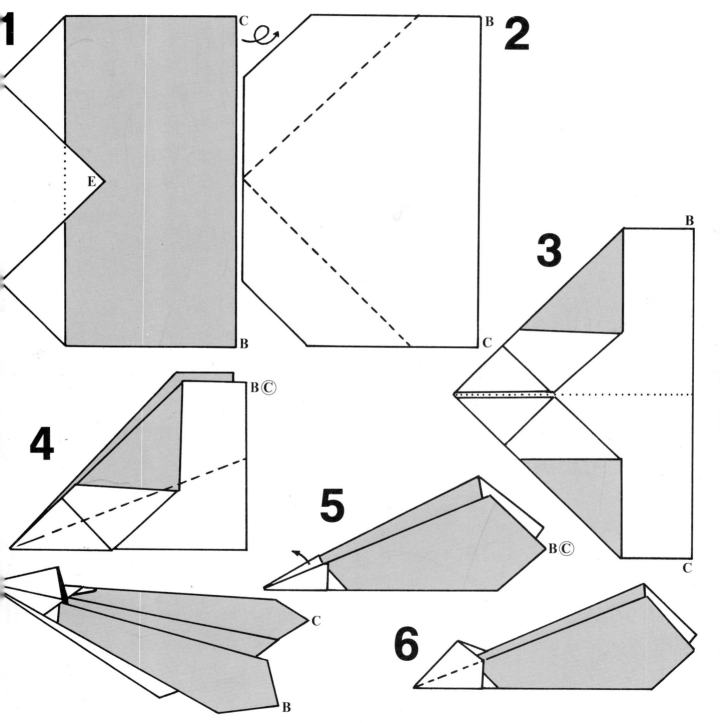

Boats

Here are two boats. Both can really be floated. There are brief directions for each boat. Test yourself. How good have you gotten at origami?

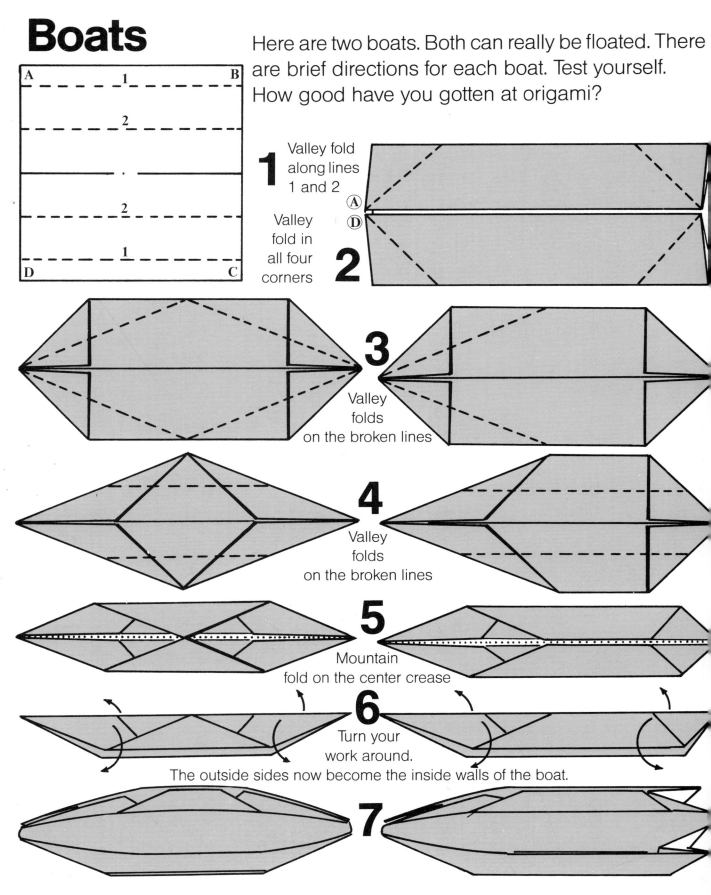

1 Valley fold along lines 1 and 2

2 Valley fold in all four corners

3 Valley folds on the broken lines

4 Valley folds on the broken lines

5 Mountain fold on the center crease

6 Turn your work around.
The outside sides now become the inside walls of the boat.

7

Tumbling Figure

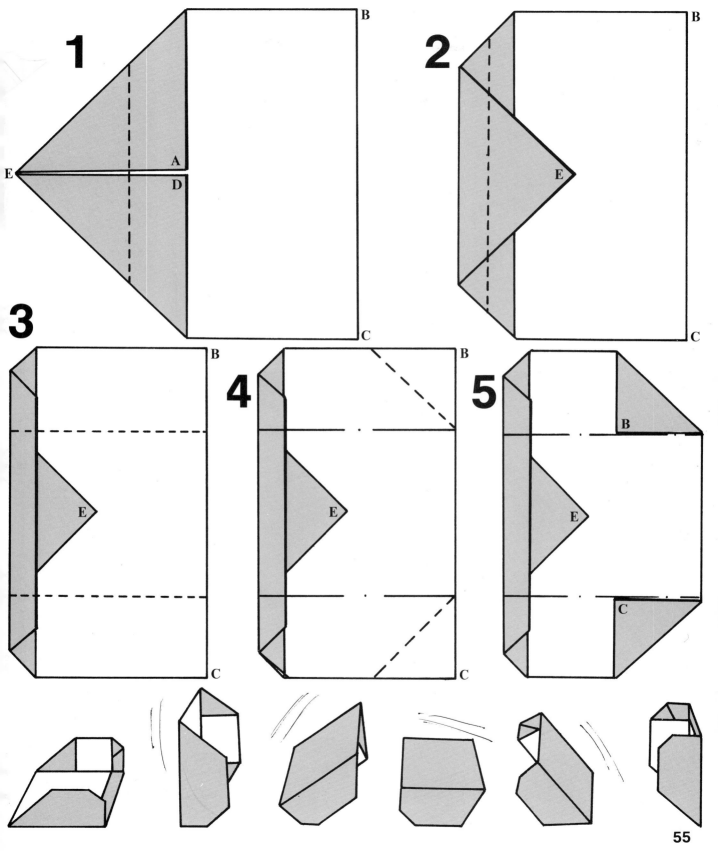

Origami Ideas

All kinds of ideas will come to you as you work on origami. Here are some suggestions.

Birthday Invitations
Simply write on the folded figures—such as boats, hats, or colored patterns. Or decorate an invitation with an origami figure.

Place Cards
Any of the standing origami figures would be good for this, including houses, birds, boats, or mice.

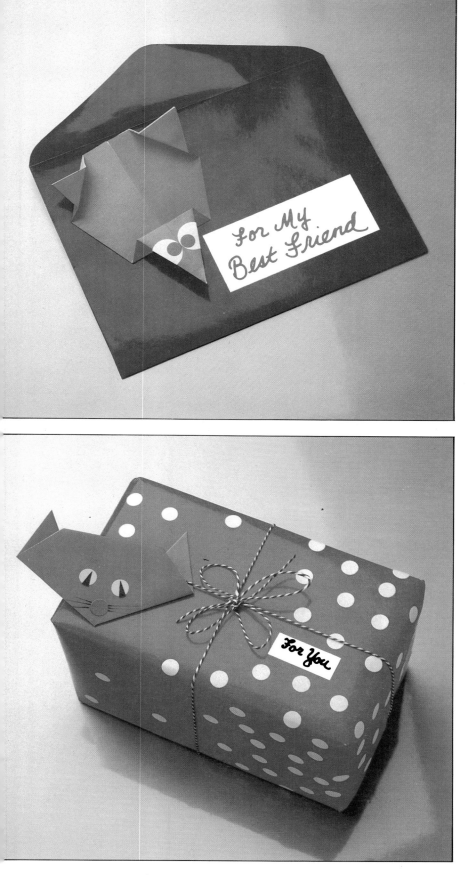

Envelope Decoration

Stick a folded origami figure in the envelope as a surprise. Decorate the outside with another figure.

Gift Wrapping

After you have wrapped a package attractively, add an origami figure or two to give it a really unique touch.

Important Rules

1. Always fold on a smooth, solid surface.

2. Make sure all folds are as straight and exact as possible.

3. Crease all folds thoroughly.

4. After each fold, return your work to the position shown in the next drawing.

5. Look not only at the drawing you are working on, but also at the one following to make sure you know how the piece should look after the new fold.

Following Directions

The drawings tell a story if you can read the directions correctly.

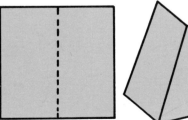
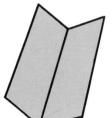

Broken line = valley fold
A valley fold is folded toward the front. When you open this fold, the crease is on the bottom like a real valley.

Broken line = reverse fold outward
(Refer to the explanation on page 35.)

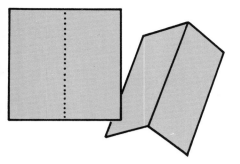

Dotted line = mountain fold

A mountain fold is folded toward the back. When opened, the crease is on the top like a mountain.

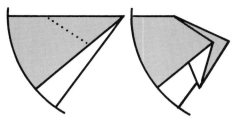

Dotted line = reverse fold inward

(Refer to the explanation on page 34.)

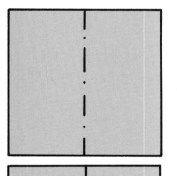

Broken dotted line = Crease only

When you see this line, make a crease, open it again, and use it as a helper line.

Incomplete line. (See broken line.)

Turned arrow = turn over

Turn the work over when you see this arrow.

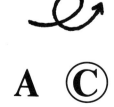

Capital letters = Corners and points

Each corner and point is "named" with a capital letter. When you first start origami, write the letters directly on the corners of your paper. It will be easier. The circled letter shows that the corner is not visible because it is in the back of the piece.

Origami Vocabulary

In the directions for the drawings, you will see certain words used repeatedly. They always have the same meaning.

the back   The back of the paper is the side that is on the table. The points and corners on the back always have circled letters.

the front   The front of the paper is the side that you are looking at.

the top   The top is the edge or corner pointing away from you.

the bottom   The bottom is the edge or corner pointing toward you.

right, left   These are the parts that lie to the right or left of the middle crease.

inside   Everything that is in between the front and back sides. Circled letters indicate inside points and corners.

outside   The back and the front of the work.

corner   Where sides join at a right angle or a wide angle.

point   A sharply pointed corner.

middle crease   Runs through the center of the paper and divides it into equal sides. A corner or a point can have a center crease.

diagonal	A crease running from one corner diagonally to the other corner.
diagonal cross	You get this when you fold both middle creases diagonally from corner to corner of your paper.
middle crease cross	You get this when you fold both middle creases parallel to the edges of the paper.
parallel	A straight line that runs in the same direction as the edge of the paper.
open	You have folded the paper. Now you open it up again.
turn around	Move your work in another direction.
turn over	Turn your work over from the front to the back.
pull	To take particular points and pull in a certain direction.
crease	The line along a fold.

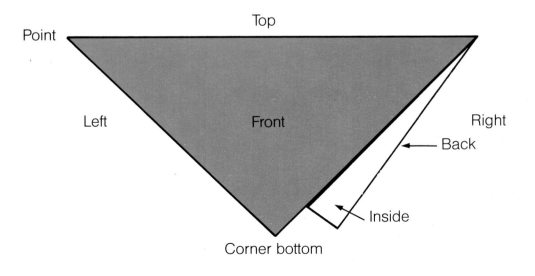

INDEX